The Order

of

the Moleben

and

the Panikhida

HOLY TRINITY PUBLICATIONS
The Printshop of St Job of Pochaev
Holy Trinity Monastery
Jordanville, New York
2021

Printed with the blessing of
His Eminence, Metropolitan Hilarion
First Hierarch of the Russian Orthodox Church
Outside of Russia

Compilation: The Order of the Moleben and the Panikhida
© 2021 Holy Trinity Monastery

PRINTSHOP OF
SAINT JOB OF POCHAEV

An imprint of

HOLY TRINITY PUBLICATIONS
Holy Trinity Monastery
Jordanville, New York 13361-0036
www.holytrinitypublications.com

ISBN: 978-0-88465-438-4 (hardback)
ISBN: 978-0-88465-441-4 (ePub)
ISBN: 978-0-88465-445-2 (Mobipocket)

Library of Congress Control Number: 2020940424

Psalms taken from *A Psalter for Prayer*, trans. David James
(Jordanville, New York: Holy Trinity Publications, 2011).

Contents

PART 1

The Order of the General Moleben

DEACON: Bless, master.

PRIEST: Blessed is our God always, now and ever, and unto the ages of ages.

CHANTERS: Amen. Glory to Thee, our God, Glory to Thee.

O Heavenly King, Comforter, Spirit of Truth, Who art everywhere present and fillest all things, Treasury of good things and Giver of life: Come and dwell in us, and cleanse us of all impurity, and save our souls, O Good One.

READER: Holy God, Holy Mighty, Holy Immortal, have mercy on us. *Thrice.*

Glory to the Father and to the Son and to the Holy Spirit, both now and ever and unto the ages of ages. Amen.

O Most Holy Trinity, have mercy on us. O Lord, blot out our sins. O Master, pardon

7

our iniquities. O Holy One, visit and heal our infirmities for Thy name's sake.

Lord, have mercy. *Thrice.*

Glory to the Father and to the Son and to the Holy Spirit, both now and ever and unto the ages of ages. Amen.

Our Father, Who art in the heavens, hallowed be Thy name. Thy kingdom come, Thy will be done, on earth as it is in heaven. Give us this day our daily bread, and forgive us our debts, as we forgive our debtors; and lead us not into temptation, but deliver us from the evil one.

PRIEST: For Thine is the kingdom, and the power, and the glory: of the Father and of the Son and of the Holy Spirit, now and ever, and unto the ages of ages.

READER: Amen.

Lord, have mercy. *Twelve times.*

Glory to the Father and to the Son and to the Holy Spirit, both now and ever, and unto the ages of ages. Amen.

O come let us worship God, our King.

O come let us worship and fall down before Christ, our King and God.

O come let us worship and fall down before Christ Himself, our King and God.

Psalm 142

O LORD, hear my prayer, consider my supplication in Thy truth; hearken unto me in Thy righteousness, and enter not into judgment with Thy servant, for before Thee shall no man living be justified. For the enemy hath persecuted my soul; he hath smitten my life down to the ground; he hath laid me in the darkness, as those that have been long dead, and my spirit is despondent within me, and my heart within me is vexed. I remembered the days of old; I mused upon all Thy works; I exercised myself in the works of Thy hands. I stretched forth my hands unto Thee; my soul gasped unto Thee as a thirsty land. Hear me soon, O Lord, for my spirit faltereth;

turn not Thy face from me, or I shall be like unto them that go down into the pit. O let me hear Thy mercy in the morning, for in Thee have I trusted; tell me, O Lord, the way that I should walk in, for I lift up my soul unto Thee. Deliver me from mine enemies, O Lord, for I have fled unto Thee. Teach me to do Thy will, for Thou art my God. Thy good Spirit shall lead me into the land of righteousness. For Thy Name's sake, O Lord, quicken me by Thy truth; Thou shalt bring my soul out of trouble. And of Thy mercy Thou shalt slay mine enemies, and destroy all them that vex my soul, for I am Thy servant.

Glory to the Father and to the Son and to the Holy Spirit, both now and ever, and unto the ages of ages. Amen.

Alleluia, alleluia, alleluia. Glory to Thee, O God. *Thrice.*

Then the deacon (or priest, if there is no deacon) says:

In the _ Tone (*the tone is the same tone of the first troparion to be chanted following*):

God is the Lord, and hath appeared unto us. Blessed is he that cometh in the name of the Lord.

DEACON: O give thanks unto the Lord, for He is good; for His mercy endureth for ever.

CHANTERS: God is the Lord, and hath appeared unto us. Blessed is he that cometh in the name of the Lord.

DEACON: All nations compassed me round about, but in the Name of the Lord have I driven them back.

CHANTERS: God is the Lord. . . .

DEACON: I shall not die, but live, and declare the works of the Lord.

CHANTERS: God is the Lord. . . .

DEACON: The stone which the builders refused, is become the head stone of the corner. This is the Lord's doing, and it is marvelous in our eyes.

CHANTERS: God is the Lord, and hath appeared unto us. Blessed is he that cometh in the name of the Lord.

Then the troparion, twice. Glory . . . Both now . . . *the Theotokion.*

If it be a moleben to the Theotokos, this troparion in the 4th Tone:

Let us sinners and lowly ones now fervently run to the Theotokos and fall before Her, crying in repentance from the depths of our souls: Taking mercy upon us, O Lady, do Thou hasten to our aid, for we perish from the multitude of our transgressions; turn not Thy servants away empty, for Thee do we have as our only hope. *Twice.*

Glory to the Father and to the Son and to the Holy Spirit, both now and ever, and unto the ages of ages. Amen.

We, unworthy ones, shall never cease, O Theotokos, to speak of Thy powers; for if Thou didst not intercede in prayer, who would deliver us from innumerable misfortunes? Who would preserve us free unto this hour? We shall not forsake Thee, O Lady, for Thou dost ever save Thy servants from all tribulations.

If the moleben is served for the sick, this troparion in the 4th Tone:

O Christ, Who alone art quick to help, manifest from on high Thy speedy visitation to Thy suffering servants, and deliver them from illness and bitter pain, and raise them up to praise and glorify Thee unceasingly, through the prayers of the Theotokos, O only Lover of mankind.

Glory to the Father and to the Son and to the Holy Spirit, both now and ever and unto the ages of ages. Amen.

As once, O Saviour, Thou didst raise up Peter's mother-in-law, and the paralyzed man who was carried on his bed, so now also, O Compassionate One, visit and heal Thy suffering servants, lying on the bed of sickness, and struck down by a mortal wound, for Thou alone didst bear the infirmities and diseases of our race, and Thou canst do all things, as One plenteous in mercy.

Then:

Psalm 50

Have mercy upon me, O God, after Thy great goodness, and according to the multitude of Thy mercies do away mine offenses. Wash me thoroughly from my wickedness, and cleanse me from my sin. For I know my fault, and my sin is ever before me. Against Thee only have I sinned, and done evil before Thee, that Thou mightiest be justified in Thy words, and prevail when Thou art judged. For behold, I was conceived in wickedness, and in sins did my mother bear me. For behold, Thou hast loved truth; the hidden and secret things of Thy wisdom hast Thou revealed unto me. Thou shalt sprinkle me with hyssop, and I shall be made clean; Thou shalt wash me, and I shall become whiter than snow. Thou shalt give joy and gladness to my hearing; the bones that have been humbled will rejoice. Turn Thy face from my sins, and put out all my misdeeds. Make me a clean heart, O God, and renew a right spirit within me. Cast me not away from Thy presence, and take not Thy Holy Spirit from me. O give me the comfort of Thy salvation, and stablish me with Thy governing Spirit. Then shall I teach Thy ways unto the wicked, and the ungodly shall be converted unto Thee. Deliver me from blood-guiltiness, O God, the God of my salvation, and my tongue shall rejoice in Thy righteousness. O Lord, open Thou my lips, and my mouth shall show forth Thy praise. For if Thou hadst desired sacrifice, I would have given it; but Thou delightest not in burnt offerings. The sacrifice unto God is a contrite spirit; a contrite and humble heart God shall not despise. O Lord, be favorable in Thy good will unto Zion, and let the walls of Jerusalem be builded up. Then shalt Thou be pleased with the sacrifice of righteousness, with oblation and whole-burnt offerings; then shall they offer young bullocks upon Thine altar.

After this, a canon may then be read, but in any case, the proper refrains are chanted:

To The Saviour

PRIEST: O Sweetest Jesus, save us!

CHANTERS: O Sweetest Jesus, save us!

PRIEST: Glory to the Father and to the Son and to the Holy Spirit.

CHANTERS: Both now and ever, and unto the ages of ages. Amen.

Repeat refrains. Then:

Deliver Thy servants from harm, O Thou Who art plenteous in mercy, for we fervently flee unto Thee, the merciful Redeemer, Master of all, the Lord Jesus.

To the Theotokos

PRIEST: O Most Holy Theotokos, save us!

CHANTERS: O Most Holy Theotokos, save us!

PRIEST: Glory to the Father and to the Son and to the Holy Spirit.

CHANTERS: Both now and ever, and unto the ages of ages. Amen.

Repeat refrains. Then:

Deliver Thy servants from harm, O Theotokos, for after God do we all flee unto Thee, as an unassailable wall and intercessor.

With loving-kindness, O All-hymned Theotokos, look upon my cruel bodily suffering, and heal the sickness of my soul.

To a Saint or to Several Saints

PRIEST: Holy Hierarch Father Nicholas, pray to God for us!

CHANTERS: Holy Hierarch Father Nicholas, pray to God for us!

Or: Holy Greatmartyr and Trophybearer George, . . . *Chanters repeat.*

Or: Holy Righteous Father John of Kronstadt, . . . *Chanters repeat.*

Or: Holy Father Herman, . . . *Chanters repeat.*

Or: Holy Blessed Xenia, . . . *Chanters repeat.*

Or: O ye holy New Martyrs and Confessors of Russia, . . . *Chanters repeat.*

PRIEST: Glory to the Father and to the Son and to the Holy Spirit.

CHANTERS: Both now and ever, and unto the ages of ages. Amen.

Repeat refrains. Then:

Pray to God for us, O holy (*N.*), for we fervently flee unto thee, the speedy helper and intercessor for our souls.

The refrains are then chanted again, thrice:

PRIEST: O Sweetest Jesus, save us!

CHANTERS: O Sweetest Jesus, save us!

PRIEST: Glory to the Father, and to the Son, and to the Holy Spirit.

CHANTERS: Both now and ever, and unto the ages of ages. Amen.

Or: O Most Holy Theotokos, save us!

Glory . . . Both now . . .

Or: Holy Hierarch Father Nicholas, pray to God for us!

Glory . . . Both now . . .

Then the proper supplicatory verse, i.e.,

Deliver Thy servants . . . *or:* Pray to God for us . . .

Here, if the priest so desires, he may read an akathist.

Then:

DEACON: Again and again, in peace let us pray to the Lord.

CHANTERS: Lord, have mercy.

DEACON: Help us, save us, have mercy on us, and keep us, O God, by Thy grace.

CHANTERS: Lord, have mercy.

DEACON: Calling to remembrance our most

holy, most pure, most blessed, glorious Lady Theotokos and Ever Virgin Mary with all the saints, let us commit ourselves and one another and all our life unto Christ our God.

CHANTERS: To Thee, O Lord.

PRIEST: For Thou art the King of Peace and the Saviour of our souls, and unto Thee do we send up glory, to the Father and to the Son and to the Holy Spirit, now and ever, and unto the ages of ages.

CHANTERS: Amen.

Then, the **DEACON:** Let us attend. Wisdom! Let us attend. The Prokeimenon in the _ Tone.
And the chanters sing the prokeimenon.
See pages 47–55.

DEACON: Let us pray to the Lord.

CHANTERS: Lord, have mercy.

PRIEST: For holy art Thou, O our God, and Thou restest in the saints, and unto Thee do we send up glory to the Father and to the Son and to the Holy Spirit, now and ever, and unto the ages of ages.

CHANTERS: Amen.

DEACON: Let every breath praise the Lord.

CHANTERS: Let every breath praise the Lord.

DEACON: Praise ye God in His saints, praise Him in the firmament of His power.

CHANTERS: Let every breath praise the Lord.

DEACON: Let every breath.

CHANTERS: Praise the Lord.

DEACON: And that He will vouchsafe unto us the hearing of the Holy Gospel, let us pray to the Lord God.

CHANTERS: Lord, have mercy. *Thrice.*

DEACON: Wisdom, Aright! Let us hear the Holy Gospel.

PRIEST: Peace be unto all.

CHANTERS: And to thy spirit.

PRIEST: The reading is from the Holy Gospel according to (*N.*)

CHANTERS: Glory to Thee, O Lord, glory to Thee.

DEACON: Let us attend.

The priest reads the appropriate Gospel (see pages 47–55 for a list of readings).

CHANTERS: Glory to Thee, O Lord, glory to Thee.

And again the refrains are chanted as before, thrice:

PRIEST: O Sweetest Jesus, save us!

CHANTERS: O Sweetest Jesus, save us!

PRIEST: Glory to the Father, and to the Son, and to the Holy Spirit.

CHANTERS: Both now and ever, and unto the ages of ages. Amen.

Or: O Most Holy Theotokos, save us!

Glory . . . Both now . . .

Or: Holy Hierarch Father Nicholas, pray to God for us!

Glory . . . Both now . . .

Then: It is truly meet to bless Thee, the Theotokos, ever-blessed and most blameless, and Mother of our God. More honorable than the Cherubim, and beyond compare more glorious than the Seraphim, Who without corruption gavest birth to God the Word, the very Theotokos, Thee do we magnify.

READER: Holy God, Holy Mighty, Holy Immortal, have mercy on us. *Thrice.*

Glory to the Father and to the Son and to the Holy Spirit, both now and ever, and unto the ages of ages. Amen.

O Most Holy Trinity, have mercy on us. O Lord, blot out our sins. O Master, pardon our iniquities. O Holy One, visit and heal our infirmities for Thy name's sake.

Lord, have mercy. *Thrice.*

Glory to the Father and to the Son and to the Holy Spirit, both now and ever, and unto the ages of ages. Amen.

Our Father, Who art in the heavens, hallowed be Thy name. Thy kingdom come, Thy will be done, on earth as it is in heaven. Give us this day our daily bread, and forgive us our debts, as we forgive our debtors; and lead us not into temptation, but deliver us from the evil one.

PRIEST: For Thine is the kingdom, and the power, and the glory, of the Father and of the Son and of the Holy Spirit, now and ever, and unto the ages of ages.

CHANTERS: Amen. *And the troparia of the feast or saint, to whom the moleben is served.*

After the troparia, the Litany:

DEACON: Have mercy on us, O God, according to Thy great mercy, we pray Thee, hearken and have mercy.

CHANTERS: Lord, have mercy. *Thrice.*

DEACON: Again we pray for our great lord and father, the Most Holy Patriarch N.; for our lord the Very Most Reverend Metropolitan N., First Hierarch of the Russian Church Abroad; for our lord the Most Reverend

(Archbishop *or* Bishop *N*.); and for all our brethren in Christ.

CHANTERS: Lord, have mercy. *Thrice.*

DEACON: Again we pray for this land, its authorities and armed forces, and for all who with faith and piety dwell therein.

CHANTERS: Lord, have mercy. *Thrice.*

DEACON: Again we pray for the God-preserved Russian land and its Orthodox people, both in the homeland and in the diaspora, and for their salvation.

CHANTERS: Lord, have mercy. *Thrice.*

DEACON: Again we pray for mercy, life, peace, health, salvation, visitation, pardon, and prosperity of the servant(*s*) of God (*N*).

CHANTERS: Lord, have mercy. *Thrice.*

DEACON: Again we pray Thee, O Lord our God, that Thou wouldst hearken unto the voice of our supplication and prayer, and have mercy on Thy servant(s) (*N*.), through Thy grace and compassions, and fulfill all their petitions, and pardon them all transgressions voluntary and involuntary, let their prayers and alms be acceptable before the throne of Thy dominion, and protect them from enemies visible and invisible, from every temptation, harm and sorrow, and deliver them from diseases, and grant them health and length of days: let us all say, O Lord, hearken and have mercy.

CHANTERS: Lord, have mercy. *Thrice.*

DEACON: Look down, O Master, Lover of mankind, with Thy merciful eye, upon Thy servants (*N.*), and hearken unto our supplication which is offered with faith, for Thou Thyself hast said: "All things whatsoever ye shall ask in prayer, believe that ye shall receive, and it will be done unto you," and again: "Ask, and it shall be given to you." Therefore we, though we be unworthy, yet hoping in Thy mercy, ask: bestow Thy kindness upon Thy servants (*N.*), and fulfill their good desires, preserve them all their days peacefully and calmly in health and length of days: let us all say, quickly hearken and graciously have mercy.

CHANTERS: Lord, have mercy. *Thrice.*

Again we pray for the people here present, who await of Thee great and abundant mercy, for all the brethren, and for all Christians.

CHANTERS: Lord, have mercy. *Thrice.*

Litany for the Sick

O Physician of souls and bodies, with compunction and broken hearts we fall down before Thee, and groaning we cry unto Thee: heal the sicknesses, heal the passions of the souls and bodies of Thy servants (*N.*), and pardon them, for Thou art kindhearted, all transgressions, voluntary and involuntary, and quickly raise them up from the bed of sickness, we pray Thee, hearken and have mercy.

CHANTERS: Lord, have mercy. *Thrice.*

O Thou Who desirest not the death of sinners, but rather that they should return to

Thee and live: spare and have mercy on Thy servants (*N.*), O Merciful One, banish sickness, drive away all passion, and all ailments, assuage chill and fever, and stretch forth Thy mighty arm, and, as Thou didst raise up Jairus's daughter from the bed of sickness, restore them to health, we pray Thee, hearken and have mercy.

CHANTERS: Lord, have mercy. *Thrice.*

O Thou Who by Thy touch didst heal Peter's mother-in-law who was sick with fever: do Thou now, in Thy loving-kindness, heal Thy terribly-suffering servants of their maladies, quickly granting them health, we fervently pray Thee, O Fount of healing, hearken and have mercy.

CHANTERS: Lord, have mercy. *Thrice.*

Again we pray to the Lord our God, that He may hearken unto the voice of the supplication of us sinners, and have mercy on His servants (*N.*), and protect them from all tribulation, harm, wrath, and necessity, and from every sickness of soul and body, granting them health with length of days, let us all say, quickly hearken and graciously have mercy.

CHANTERS: Lord, have mercy. *Thrice.*

Again we pray that this city (*or* this village) and this holy temple (if in a monastery: this holy monastery), and every city and country, may be preserved from famine, pestilence, earthquake, flood, fire, the sword, foreign invasion, and from civil war; that our good God, the Lover of mankind, may be gracious and favorable, that He may take away all the wrath stirred up against us, and deliver us from His righteous threatening which hangeth over us, and have mercy on us.

CHANTERS: Lord, have mercy. *Thrice.*

Again we pray also that the Lord God may hearken unto the voice of the supplication of us sinners, and have mercy on us.

CHANTERS: Lord, have mercy. *Thrice.*

PRIEST: Hearken unto us, O God our Saviour, Thou hope of all the ends of the earth and of them that be far off at sea; and be merciful, be merciful, O Master, regarding our sins, and have mercy on us; for a merciful God art Thou, and the Lover of mankind, and unto Thee do we send up glory: to the Father and to the Son and to the Holy Spirit, now and ever, and unto the ages of ages.

CHANTERS: Amen.

After the litany, a prayer is said to whomever the moleben is served.

For every request to the Saviour, the deacon says:

Let us pray to the Lord.

CHANTERS: Lord, have mercy.

Then the priest reads a prayer to the Saviour, or this one for the ailing.

A Prayer for the Ailing

O Master Almighty, O Holy King, Who chastenest but destroyest not, Who strengthenest the downcast, and settest aright the fallen, Who correctest the bodily afflictions of mankind: we pray Thee, O our God, visit Thine infirm servants *(N.)* with Thy mercy, pardon them every transgression, voluntary and involuntary. Yea, O Lord, send down Thy healing power from heaven, touch the body, quench the fever, subdue the passions and every subtle infirmity. Be the healer of Thy servants *(N.)*, raise them up whole and complete from the couch of sickness and from the bed of suffering; grant them unto Thy Church as well-pleasing and doers of Thy will. For Thine it is to show mercy and to save us, O our God, and unto Thee do we send up glory: to the Father and to the Son and to the Holy Spirit, now and ever, and unto the ages of ages.

CHANTERS: Amen.

If it be to the Most Holy Theotokos, the deacon says:

To the Most Holy Lady Virgin Theotokos, let us pray.

CHANTERS: O Most Holy Theotokos, save us!

The Prayer

O our Most Blessed Queen, O Theotokos our hope, guardian of orphans, intercessor for strangers, joy of the sorrowful, protectress of the wronged: Thou seest our misfortune, Thou seest our affliction; help us, for we are infirm; feed us, for we are strangers. Thou knowest our offenses: absolve them as Thou wilt, for we have no other help beside Thee, no other intercessor, nor good consoler, except Thee, O Mother of God. Do Thou preserve and protect us unto the ages of ages.

CHANTERS: Amen.

DEACON: Wisdom!

PRIEST: O Most Holy Theotokos, save us!

CHANTERS: More honorable than the Cherubim and beyond compare more glorious than the Seraphim, Who without corruption gavest birth to God the Word, the very Theotokos, Thee do we magnify.

PRIEST: Glory to Thee, O Christ God, our hope, glory to Thee.

CHANTERS: Glory to the Father and to the Son and to the Holy Spirit, both now and ever, and unto the ages of ages. Amen.

Lord, have mercy *Thrice.*

Father (Master), bless.

The Dismissal

PRIEST: May Christ our true God, through the intercessions of His most pure Mother, of our holy and God-bearing fathers (*N.*) (*to whom the moleben was served*); and of all the saints, have mercy on us and save us, for He is good and the Lover of mankind.

CHANTERS: Amen.

And if "Many Years" is to be chanted:

DEACON: A prosperous and peaceful life, health, salvation, and good success in all things, grant, O Lord, unto Thy servants (*N.*), and preserve them for many years.

CHANTERS: God grant you many years! *Thrice.*

The Paschal Moleben as Served During Bright Week

The full Bright Week beginning with the Paschal verses:

THE PRIEST: Blessed is our God . . .

CHANTERS: Amen.

THE PRIEST: Christ is risen . . . T*hrice.*

CHANTERS: Christ is risen . . . *Thrice.*

THE PRIEST: Let God arise and let His enemies be scattered, and let them that hate Him flee from before His face.

CHANTERS: Christ is risen . . . *Once.*

THE PRIEST: As smoke vanisheth, so let them vanish, as wax melteth before the fire.

CHANTERS: Christ is risen . . . *Once.*

THE PRIEST: So let sinners perish at the presence of God, and let the righteous be glad.

CHANTERS: Christ is risen . . . *Once.*

THE PRIEST: This is the day which the Lord hath made; let us rejoice and be glad therein.

CHANTERS: Christ is risen . . . *Once.*

THE PRIEST: Glory to the Father, and to the Son, and to the Holy Spirit.

CHANTERS: Christ is risen . . . *Once.*

THE PRIEST: Both now and ever, and unto the ages of ages. Amen.

CHANTERS: Christ is risen . . . *Once.*

THE PRIEST: Christ is risen from the dead, trampling down death by death . . .

CHANTERS: . . . and on those in the tombs bestowing life.

Then: Glory . . . Both now . . .

The Hypakoe

Forestalling the dawn, the women came with Mary and found the stone rolled away from the sepulcher and heard from the angel: Why seek ye among the dead, as though He were mortal, Him Who liveth in everlasting light?

Behold the graveclothes. Go quickly and proclaim to the world that the Lord is risen and hath slain death, for He is the Son of God, Who saveth mankind.

If you desire to include a canon for a saint, say first the troparion of the saint, once.

Glory . . . Both now . . . Forestalling the dawn . . .

Thereafter, the Paschal Canon, with its eirmoi, on 6.

REFRAIN: Christ is risen from the dead . . . (*and for the saint, if it be done*). *Then the Katavasia. After the 3rd and 6th Odes:* Save thy servants from harm . . .

After the 6th Ode: the Kontakion and the Ekos of Pascha.

The Kontakion

Though Thou didst descend into the grave, O Immortal One, yet didst Thou destroy the power of hades and didst arise as victor, O Christ God, calling to the myrrh-bearing women: Rejoice! and giving peace unto Thine apostles: Thou Who dost grant resurrection to the fallen.

The Ekos of Pascha

The myrrh-bearing maidens forestalled the dawn, seeking, as it were day, the Sun that was before the sun and Who had once set in the tomb, and they cried out one to another: O friends! Come, let us anoint with spices the life-bringing and buried Body, the Flesh that raised up fallen Adam, that now lieth in the tomb. Let us go, let us hasten, like the Magi, and let us worship and offer myrrh as a gift to Him Who is wrapped now not in swaddling clothes but in a shroud. And let us weep and cry aloud: O Master, arise, Thou Who dost grant resurrection to the fallen.

Then the Prokeimenon in the 8th Tone: This is the day which the Lord hath made; let us rejoice and be glad therein. *Stichos:* O give thanks unto the Lord, for He is good, for His mercy endureth for ever.

Then the prokeimenon of the saint. The Gospel according to Luke, Lection 114 (24:36–53); then the reading for the saint. After the 9th Ode, instead of "It is truly meet" sing the Eirmos: Shine, shine O new Jerusalem. *Then:* Christ is risen . . . *Thrice. Followed by the Hypakoe:* Forestalling the dawn . . . Glory . . . *the troparion of the saint.* Both now . . .

The Kontakion

Though Thou didst descend into the grave, O Immortal One, yet didst Thou destroy the power of hades and didst arise as victor, O Christ God, calling to the myrrh-bearing women: Rejoice! and giving peace unto Thine apostles: Thou Who dost grant resurrection to the fallen.

DEACON: Have mercy on us, O God, according to Thy great mercy, we pray Thee, hearken and have mercy.

CHANTERS: Lord, have mercy. *Thrice.*

DEACON: Again we pray for our great lord and father, the Most Holy Patriarch N.; for our lord the Very Most Reverend Metropolitan N., First Hierarch of the Russian Church Abroad; for our lord the Most Reverend (Archbishop *or* Bishop *N.*); and for all our brethren in Christ.

CHANTERS: Lord, have mercy. *Thrice.*

DEACON: Again we pray for this land, its authorities and armed forces, and for all who with faith and piety dwell therein.

CHANTERS: Lord, have mercy. *Thrice.*

DEACON: Again we pray for the God-preserved Russian land and its Orthodox people, both in the homeland and in the diaspora, and for their salvation.

CHANTERS: Lord, have mercy. *Thrice.*

DEACON: Again we pray for mercy, life, peace, health, salvation, visitation, pardon, and prosperity of the servant(s) of God (*N*).

CHANTERS: Lord, have mercy. *Thrice.*

DEACON: Again we pray Thee, O Lord our God, that Thou wouldst hearken unto the voice of our supplication and prayer, and have mercy on Thy servant(s) (*N.*), through Thy grace and compassions, and fulfill all their petitions, and pardon them all transgressions voluntary and involuntary; let their prayers and alms be acceptable before the throne of Thy dominion, and protect them from enemies visible and invisible, from every temptation, harm and sorrow, and deliver them from diseases, and grant them health and length of days: let us all say, O Lord, hearken and have mercy.

CHANTERS: Lord, have mercy. *Thrice.*

DEACON: Look down, O Master, Lover of mankind, with Thy merciful eye, upon Thy servants (*N.*), and hearken unto our supplication which is offered with faith, for Thou Thyself hast said: "All things whatsoever ye shall ask in prayer, believe that ye shall receive, and it will be done unto you," and again: "Ask, and it shall be given to you." Therefore we, though we be unworthy, yet hoping in Thy mercy, ask: bestow Thy kindness upon Thy servants (*N.*), and fulfill their good desires, preserve them all their days peacefully and calmly in health and length of days: let us all say, quickly hearken and graciously have mercy.

CHANTERS: Lord, have mercy. *Thrice.*

Again we pray for the people here present, who await of Thee great and abundant mercy, for all the brethren, and for all Christians.

CHANTERS: Lord, have mercy. *Thrice.*

Litany for the Sick

O Physician of souls and bodies, with compunction and broken hearts we fall down before Thee, and groaning we cry unto Thee: heal the sicknesses, heal the passions of the souls and bodies of Thy servants (*N.*), and pardon them, for Thou art kindhearted, all transgressions, voluntary and involuntary, and quickly raise them up from the bed of sickness, we pray Thee, hearken and have mercy.

CHANTERS: Lord, have mercy. *Thrice.*

O Thou Who desirest not the death of sinners, but rather that they should return to Thee and live: spare and have mercy on Thy servants (*N.*), O Merciful One, banish sickness, drive away all passion, and all ailments, assuage chill and fever, and stretch forth Thy mighty arm, and, as Thou didst raise up Jairus's daughter from the bed of sickness, restore them to health, we pray Thee, hearken and have mercy.

CHANTERS: Lord, have mercy. *Thrice.*

O Thou Who by Thy touch didst heal Peter's mother-in-law who was sick with fever: do Thou now, in Thy loving-kindness, heal Thy terribly-suffering servants of their maladies, quickly granting them health, we fervently pray Thee, O Fount of healing, hearken and have mercy.

CHANTERS: Lord, have mercy. *Thrice.*

Again we pray to the Lord our God, that He may hearken unto the voice of the supplication of us sinners, and have mercy on His servants (*N.*), and protect them from all tribulation, harm, wrath, and necessity, and from every sickness of soul and body, granting them health with length of days, let us all say, quickly hearken and graciously have mercy.

CHANTERS: Lord, have mercy. *Thrice.*

Again we pray that this city (*or* this village) and this holy temple (if in a monastery: this holy monastery), and every city and country, may be preserved from famine, pestilence, earthquake, flood, fire, the sword, foreign invasion, and from civil war; that our good God, the Lover of mankind, may be gracious and favorable, that He may take away all the wrath stirred up against us, and deliver us from His righteous threatening which hangeth over us, and have mercy on us.

CHANTERS: Lord, have mercy. *Thrice.*

Again we pray also that the Lord God may hearken unto the voice of the supplication of us sinners, and have mercy on us.

CHANTERS: Lord, have mercy. *Thrice.*

PRIEST: Hearken unto us, O God our Saviour, Thou hope of all the ends of the earth and of them that be far off at sea; and be merciful, be merciful, O Master, regarding our sins, and have mercy on us; for a merciful God art Thou, and the Lover of mankind, and unto Thee do we send up glory: to the Father and to the Son and to the Holy Spirit, now and ever, and unto the ages of ages.

CHANTERS: Amen.

Thereafter, the priest: Wisdom! *Chanters:* Christ is risen ... *Thrice. Then, the priest (instead of: Glory to Thee, O Christ God . . .):* Christ is risen from the dead, trampling down death by death . . . *Chanters:* . . . and on those in the tombs bestowing life.

And the dismissal with the cross is said thus: May Christ our true God, Who rose from the dead . . . *according as it is written at the conclusion of the Paschal Matins. Thereafter the priest:* Christ is risen! *Thrice. Chanters:* Truly He is risen! *Thrice. And again, Chanters:* Christ is risen . . . *Thrice.*

Then: And unto us hath He granted life eternal; wherefore, we worship His Resurrection on the third day.

A Prayer for the Living

Save, O Lord, and have mercy on all Orthodox Christians and those that lead an Orthodox life in every place of Thy dominion. Grant unto them, O Lord, peace of soul and bodily health. Pardon them every sin, voluntary and involuntary, through the intercessions of Thy Most Pure Mother and all Thy saints, and have mercy on me, the wretched one.

The Prokeimena and the Gospel Readings

For every request to the Saviour

PROKEIMENON, TONE 4: O Lord, hear my prayer, consider my supplication in Thy truth.

VERSE: O praise the Lord, for the Lord is good.

GOSPEL: Matthew, Lection 20 (7:7–11).

For the Most Holy Theotokos

PROKEIMENON, TONE 4: I will remember Thy name in every generation and generation.

VERSE: My heart hath poured forth a good Word.

GOSPEL: Luke, Lection 4 (1:39–49,56).

For the Ailing

PROKEIMENON, TONE 4: Have mercy on me, O Lord, for I am weak; O Lord, heal me, for my bones are vexed.

VERSE: For in death no man remembereth Thee.

GOSPEL: Matthew, Lection 25 (8:5–13).

For the Angels

PROKEIMENON, TONE 4: Who maketh His angels spirits, and His ministers a flaming fire.

VERSE: Bless the Lord, O my soul; O Lord my God, Thou hast been magnified exceedingly.

GOSPEL: Luke, Lection 51 (10:16–21); *or:* Matthew, Lection 52 (13:24–30, 36 beginning at the words "and His disciples," and continuing through verse 43).

For a Prophet or Prophets

PROKEIMENON, TONE 4: Thou art a priest for ever, after the order of Melchizedek.

VERSE: The Lord said unto my Lord, Sit Thou at my right hand, until I make Thine enemies the footstool of Thy feet.

GOSPEL: Matthew, Lection 96 (23:29–39); *or:* Luke, Lection 62 (11:47–12:1).

For an Apostle

PROKEIMENON, TONE 4: Their sound is gone out into all the earth, and their words unto the ends of the world.

VERSE: The heavens declare the glory of God, and the firmament showeth His handy-work.

GOSPEL: Matthew, Lection 34 (9:36–10:8).

For several Apostles

PROKEIMENON, TONE 4: Their sound is gone out into all the earth, and their words unto the ends of the world.

VERSE: The heavens declare the glory of God, and the firmament showeth His handy-work.

GOSPEL: Luke, Lection 50 (lo:1–15); *or:* Luke, Lection 34 (10:16–21).

For one Hierarch

PROKEIMENON, TONE 1: My mouth shall speak wisdom, and the meditation of my heart shall be of understanding.

VERSE: Hear this, all ye nations; take heed, all ye that dwell in the world.

GOSPEL: John, Lection 36 (10:9–16).

For several Hierarchs

PROKEIMENON, TONE 4: Precious in the sight of the Lord is the death of His saints.

VERSE: What shall I render unto the Lord, for all that He hath rendered unto me?

GOSPEL: Matthew, Lection 11 (5:14–19); *or:* John, Lection 35 (10:1–9).

For Monks and Fools-for-Christ

PROKEIMENON, TONE 4: Precious in the sight of the Lord is the death of His saints.

VERSE: What shall I ender unto the Lord for all that He hath rendered unto me?

GOSPEL: Matthew, Lection 43 (11:27–30); *or:* Luke, Lection 24 (6:17–23) (through the word "heaven").

For a Martyr

PROKEIMENON, TONE 4: The righteous man shall rejoice in the Lord, and shall put his trust in Him.

VERSE: Give ear, Lord, unto my prayer, and heed the voice of my supplication.

GOSPEL: Luke, Lection 63 (12:2–12); *or:* John, Lection 52 (15:17–16:2).

For several Martyrs

PROKEIMENON, TONE 4: Unto the saints that are in His land hath the Lord made wonderful all His desires in them.

VERSE: I foresaw the Lord always before me, for He is on my right hand, that I should not be moved.

GOSPEL: Matthew, Lection 36 (10:16–22); *or:* Luke, Lection 106 (21:12–19).

For a Hieromartyr

PROKEIMENON, TONE 8: The saints shall boast in glory, and they will rejoice upon their beds.

VERSE: Sing unto the Lord a new song; His praise is in the church of the saints.

GOSPEL: Luke, Lection 67 (12:32–40).

For several Hieromartyrs

PROKEIMENON, TONE 8: The saints shall boast in glory, and they will rejoice upon their beds.

VERSE: Sing unto the Lord a new song; His praise is in the church of the saints.

GOSPEL: Luke, Lection 24 (6:17–23 through the word "heaven"); *or:* Luke, Lection 52 (10: 22–24); *or:* Luke, Lection 77 (14:25–35).

For a Monk-martyr

PROKEIMENON, TONE 8: The saints shall boast in glory, and they will rejoice upon their beds.

VERSE: Sing unto the Lord a new song; His praise is in the church of the saints.

GOSPEL: Mark, Lection 37 (8:34 beginning: "He [the Lord] said unto them, 'Whosoever . . .'" through 9:1).

For several Monk-martyrs

PROKEIMENON, TONE 4: Unto the saints that are in His land hath the Lord made wonderful all His desires in them.

VERSE: I foresaw the Lord always before me, for He is on my right hand, that I should not be moved.

GOSPEL: Matthew, Lection 38 (10: 32–11:1); *or:* Luke, Lection 64 (12: 8–12).

For Women-martyrs

PROKEIMENON, TONE 4: Wonderful is God in His saints, the God of Israel.

VERSE: In churches bless ye God, the Lord from the fountains of Israel.

GOSPEL: Matthew, Lection 62 (15: 21–28); *or:* Mark, Lection 21 (5:24 beginning: At that time: "a great multitude followed Him" through verse 34).

For Nun Saints

PROKEIMENON, TONE 4: Wonderful is God in His saints, the God of Israel.

VERSE: In churches bless ye God, the Lord from the fountains of Israel.

GOSPEL: Matthew, Lection 104 (25:1–13); *or:* Luke, Lection 64 (7:36–50).

For Confessors

PROKEIMENON, TONE 8: The saints shall boast in glory, and they will rejoice upon their beds.

VERSE: Sing unto the Lord a new song; His praise is in the church of the saints.

GOSPEL: Luke, Lection 64 (12: 8–12).

For Unmercenaries

PROKEIMENON, TONE 4: Unto the saints that are in His land hath the Lord made wonderful all His desires in them.

VERSE: I foresaw the Lord always before me, for He is on my right hand, that I should not be moved.

GOSPEL: Matthew, Lection 34 (9:36–10:8).

For the New Martyrs and
Confessors of Russia

PROKEIMENON, TONE 4: For Thy sake, O Lord, we are killed all the day long.

VERSE: We are accounted sheep for the slaughter.

GOSPEL: Matthew, Lection 36 (10:16–22).

PART 2

The Panikhida or the Memorial Service for the Dead

THE PRIEST: Blessed is our God always, now and ever, and unto the ages of ages.

CHANTERS: Amen.

Holy God, Holy Mighty, Holy Immortal, have mercy on us. *Thrice.*

READER: Glory to the Father and to the Son and to the Holy Spirit, both now and ever, and unto the ages of ages. Amen.

O Most Holy Trinity, have mercy on us. O Lord, blot out our sins. O Master, pardon our iniquities. O Holy One, visit and heal our infirmities for Thy name's sake.

Lord, have mercy. *Thrice.*

Glory to the Father and to the Son and to the Holy Spirit, both now and ever, and unto the ages of ages. Amen.

Our Father, Who art in the heavens,

hallowed be Thy name. Thy kingdom come, Thy will be done, on earth as it is in heaven. Give us this day our daily bread, and forgive us our debts, as we forgive our debtors; and lead us not into temptation, but deliver us from the evil one.

PRIEST: For Thine is the kingdom and the power and the glory, of the Father and of the Son and of the Holy Spirit, now and ever, and unto the ages of ages.

READER: Amen.

Lord, have mercy. *Twelve times.*

Glory to the Father and to the Son and to the Holy Spirit, both now and ever, and unto the ages of ages. Amen.

O come let us worship God, our King.

O come let us worship and fall down before Christ, our King and God.

O come let us worship and fall down before Christ Himself, our King and God.

Psalm 90

Whoso dwelleth in the help of the Most High shall abide in the shelter of the God of heaven. He will say unto the Lord, Thou art my defender, and my refuge, my God, and I will trust in Him. For He shall deliver thee from the snare of the hunter, and from every mutinous word. With His wings will He overshadow thee, and thou shalt be safe under His feathers; His truth shall compass thee round about like a shield. Thou shalt not be afraid for any terror by night, nor for the arrow that flieth by day; for the thing that walketh in darkness, for sickness, or the demon of noonday. A thousand shall fall beside thee, and ten thousand at thy right hand, but unto thee it shall not come nigh. But thou shalt behold with thine eyes, and see the reward of sinners. For Thou, Lord, art my hope; thou hast made the Most High thy refuge. There shall no evil happen unto thee, neither shall any plague come nigh thy dwelling. For He shall give His angels charge over thee, to keep thee in all thy ways. They shall bear thee in their hands, that thou hurt not thy foot against a stone. Thou shalt step upon the asp and basilisk; the lion and the serpent shalt thou tread under thy feet. Because he hath set his hope upon Me, therefore will I deliver him; I will shelter him, because he hath known My Name. He shall call upon Me, and I will hear him; yea, I am with him in trouble, I will deliver him, and bring him to glory. With long life will I satisfy him, and show him My salvation.

Glory to the Father and to the Son and to the Holy Spirit, both now and ever, and unto the ages of ages. Amen.

Alleluia, alleluia, alleluia. Glory to Thee, O God. *Thrice.*

Thereafter, the Litany:

DEACON: In peace let us pray to the Lord.

CHANTERS: Lord, have mercy.

For the peace from above, and the salvation of our souls, let us pray to the Lord.

CHANTERS: Lord, have mercy.

DEACON: For the remission of the sins of those who have departed this life in blessed memory, let us pray to the Lord.

CHANTERS: Lord, have mercy.

DEACON: For the ever-memorable servant(s) of God (*N.*); for his/her (*or* their) repose, tranquility and blessed memory, let us pray to the Lord.

CHANTERS: Lord, have mercy.

DEACON: That He will pardon them every transgression, both voluntary and involuntary, let us pray to the Lord.

CHANTERS: Lord, have mercy.

DEACON: That they may appear uncondemned before the dread throne of the Lord of glory, let us pray to the Lord.

CHANTERS: Lord, have mercy.

DEACON: For them that mourn and grieve, who look for the consolation of Christ, let us pray to the Lord.

CHANTERS: Lord, have mercy.

DEACON: That He will release them from all sickness, sorrow, and sighing, and settle them where the light of God's countenance shall visit them, let us pray to the Lord.

CHANTERS: Lord, have mercy.

DEACON: That the Lord our God will commit their souls to a place of light, a place of green pasture, a place of repose, where all the righteous dwell, let us pray to the Lord.

CHANTERS: Lord, have mercy.

DEACON: That they may be numbered with them that are in the bosom of Abraham and Isaac and Jacob, let us pray to the Lord.

CHANTERS: Lord, have mercy.

DEACON: That we may be delivered from all tribulation, wrath, and necessity, let us pray to the Lord.

CHANTERS: Lord, have mercy.

DEACON: Help us, save us, have mercy on us, and keep us, O God, by Thy grace.

CHANTERS: Lord, have mercy.

DEACON: Having asked for the mercy of God, the kingdom of heaven, and the remission of sins both for them and for ourselves, let us commit ourselves and one another and all our life unto Christ our God.

CHANTERS: To Thee, O Lord.

PRIEST: For Thou art the resurrection and the life and the repose of Thy departed servant(s) (N.), O Christ our God, and unto Thee do we send up glory, together with Thine unoriginate Father, and Thy most holy and good and life-creating Spirit, now and ever, and unto the ages of ages.

CHANTERS: Amen.

DEACON: Alleluia in the 8th Tone:

Blessed is the man whom Thou hast chosen and taken unto Thyself, O Lord.

CHANTERS: Alleluia, alleluia, alleluia.

DEACON: Their remembrance is unto generation and generation.

CHANTERS: Alleluia, alleluia, alleluia.

DEACON: Their souls shall dwell among good things.

CHANTERS: Alleluia, alleluia, alleluia.

Then the troparion, same tone:

O Thou Who by the depth of Thy wisdom dost provide all things out of love for man, and grantest unto all, that which is profitable, O only Creator: Grant rest, O Lord, to the soul(s) of Thy servant(s); for in Thee hath he/she (*or,* have they) placed his/her (their) hope, O our Creator and Fashioner and God.

Glory to the Father and to the Son and to the Holy Spirit, both now and ever, and unto the ages of ages. Amen.

THEOTOKION: In Thee we have a wall and a haven, and an intercessor acceptable to

God Whom Thou didst bear, O Theotokos Unwedded, salvation of the faithful.

Then the following troparia are sung by the chanters in the 5th Tone ("Blessed are the Blameless")

REFRAIN: Blessed art Thou, O Lord, teach me Thy statutes.

The Choir of the saints have found the fountain of life and the door of paradise. May I also find the way through repentance. I am the lost sheep, call me back, O Saviour, and save me.

REFRAIN: Blessed art Thou, O Lord, teach me Thy statutes.

Ye that have preached the Lamb of God, and like lambs were slain, O holy ones, translated unto life unaging and everlasting, fervently entreat Him, O ye martyrs, to grant us forgiveness of our sins.

REFRAIN: Blessed art Thou, O Lord, teach me Thy statutes.

Ye that have trod the narrow way of sorrow; all ye that in life have taken up the Cross as a yoke, and have followed Me in faith, come, enjoy the honors and heavenly crowns which I have prepared for you.

REFRAIN: Blessed art Thou, O Lord, teach me Thy statutes.

I am an image of Thine ineffable glory, though I bear the wounds of sin; take compassion on Thy creature, O Master, and cleanse me by Thy loving-kindness; and grant me the desired fatherland, making me again a dweller of paradise.

REFRAIN: Blessed art Thou, O Lord, teach me Thy statutes.

O Thou Who of old didst create me out of nothing, and didst honor me with Thy divine image, but because of my transgression of the commandment didst return me again unto the earth, whence I was taken: Raise me up according to Thy likeness, that I may be fashioned in the ancient beauty.

REFRAIN: Blessed art Thou, O Lord, teach me Thy statutes.

Give rest, O God, to Thy servant(s) and commit him/her (them) to paradise, where the choirs of the saints, O Lord, and of the righteous shine as the stars; give rest unto Thy departed servant(s), disregarding all his/her (their) sins.

Glory to the Father and to the Son and to the Holy Spirit.

TRIADICON: Let us piously hymn the triple radiance of the one Godhead, crying aloud: Holy art Thou, O unoriginate Father, co-unoriginate Son, and Divine Spirit; enlighten us who with faith worship Thee, and snatch us from the eternal fire.

Both now and ever, and unto the ages of ages. Amen.

THEOTOKION: Rejoice, O Pure One, who gavest birth to God in the flesh for the salvation of all, and through Whom mankind hath found salvation; through Thee may we find paradise, O Theotokos, pure and blessed.

Alleluia, alleluia, alleluia. Glory to Thee, O God. *Thrice.*

DEACON: Again and again, in peace let us pray to the Lord.

CHANTERS: Lord, have mercy.

DEACON: Again we pray for the repose of the soul(s) of the departed servant(s) of God *(N.)*, and that he/she (they) may be forgiven every transgression, both voluntary and involuntary.

CHANTERS: Lord, have mercy.

DEACON: That the Lord God commit their souls to where the righteous repose.

CHANTERS: Lord, have mercy.

DEACON: The mercy of God, the kingdom of heaven, and the remission of their sins, let us ask of Christ, the Immortal King and our God.

CHANTERS: Grant this, O Lord.

DEACON: Let us pray to the Lord.

CHANTERS: Lord, have mercy.

PRIEST'S EXCLAMATION: For Thou art the resurrection, and the life, and the repose of Thy departed servant(s) *(N.)*, O Christ our God, and unto Thee do we send up glory, together with Thine unoriginate Father, and Thy most holy and good and life-creating Spirit, now and ever, and unto the ages of ages.

CHANTERS: Amen.

Then, the Sessional Hymn, 5th Tone:

Give rest with the righteous, O our Saviour, unto Thy servants, and settle them in Thy courts, according as it is written, disregarding, as Thou art good, their transgressions voluntary and involuntary, and all they committed either knowingly or unknowingly, O Lover of mankind.

Glory to the Father and to the Son and to the Holy Spirit, both now and ever, and unto the ages of ages. Amen.

THEOTOKION: O Christ God, Who didst shine forth unto the world from the Virgin, manifesting through Her the sons of light, have mercy on us.

Then this set of refrains from the canon, twice:

PRIEST: Give rest, O Lord, to the soul(s) of Thy servant(s) who hath (have) fallen asleep.

CHANTERS: Give rest, O Lord, to the soul(s) of Thy servant(s) who hath (have) fallen asleep.

PRIEST: Glory to the Father and to the Son and to the Holy Spirit.

CHANTERS: Both now and ever, and unto the ages of ages. Amen.

The Eirmos, Ode III, 6th Tone:

There is none holy as Thou, O Lord my God, Who hast exalted the horn of Thy faithful, O Good One, and hast established us upon the rock of Thy confession.

DEACON: Again and again, in peace let us pray to the Lord.

CHANTERS: Lord, have mercy.

DEACON: Again we pray for the repose of the soul(s) of the departed servant(s) of God (*N.*), and that he/she (they) may be forgiven every transgression, both voluntary and involuntary.

CHANTERS: Lord, have mercy.

DEACON: That the Lord God commit their souls to where the righteous repose.

CHANTERS: Lord, have mercy.

DEACON: The mercy of God, the kingdom of heaven, and the remission of their sins, let us ask of Christ, the Immortal King and our God.

CHANTERS: Grant this, O Lord.

DEACON: Let us pray to the Lord.

CHANTERS: Lord, have mercy.

PRIEST'S EXCLAMATION: For Thou art the resurrection, and the life, and the repose of Thy departed servant*(s)* (*N.*), O Christ our God, and unto Thee do we send up glory, together with Thine unoriginate Father, and Thy most holy and good and life-creating Spirit, now and ever, and unto the ages of ages.

CHANTERS: Amen.

Then the Sessional Hymn, 6th Tone:

Truly all things are vanity, and life is but a shadow and a dream; for in vain doth every one born of earth disquiet himself, as saith the Scripture: when we have acquired the world, then do we take up our abode in the grave, where together are both kings and beggars. Wherefore, O Christ God, give rest to the departed, as Thou art the Lover of mankind.

Glory to the Father and to the Son and to the Holy Spirit, both now and ever, and unto the ages of ages. Amen.

THEOTOKION: O All-holy Theotokos, in my lifetime forsake me not, to human protection entrust me not, but do Thou Thyself defend and have mercy on me.

Then this set of refrains from the canon, thrice:

PRIEST: Give rest, O Lord, to the soul(s) of Thy servant(s) who hath (have) fallen asleep.

CHANTERS: Give rest, O Lord, to the soul(s) of Thy servant(s) who hath (have) fallen asleep.

PRIEST: Glory to the Father and to the Son and to the Holy Spirit.

CHANTERS: Both now and ever, and unto the ages of ages. Amen.

The Eirmos, Ode VI:

Beholding the sea of life surging with the storm of temptations, I run to Thy calm haven and cry unto Thee: Raise up my life from corruption, O Greatly-merciful One.

DEACON: Again and again, in peace let us pray to the Lord.

CHANTERS: Lord, have mercy.

DEACON: Again we pray for the repose of the soul(s) of the departed servant(s) of God (*N.*), and that he/she (they) may be forgiven every transgression, both voluntary and involuntary.

CHANTERS: Lord, have mercy.

DEACON: That the Lord God commit their souls to where the righteous repose.

CHANTERS: Lord, have mercy.

DEACON: The mercy of God, the kingdom of heaven, and the remission of their sins, let us ask of Christ, the Immortal King and our God.

CHANTERS: Grant this, O Lord.

DEACON: Let us pray to the Lord.

CHANTERS: Lord, have mercy.

PRIEST'S EXCLAMATION: For Thou art the resurrection, and the life, and the repose of Thy departed servant*(s)* (*N.*), O Christ our God, and unto Thee do we send up glory, together with Thine unoriginate Father, and Thy most holy and good and life-creating Spirit, now and ever, and unto the ages of ages.

CHANTERS: Amen.

Then the kontakion, 8th Tone:

With the saints give rest, O Christ, to the souls of Thy servants, where there is neither sickness, nor sorrow, nor sighing, but life everlasting.

EKOS: Thou alone art immortal, Who didst create and fashion man; but we mortals were formed of earth, and unto earth shall we return, as Thou Who madest me didst command and say unto me: For earth thou art and unto earth shalt thou return, whither all we mortals are going, making as a funeral dirge the song: Alleluia, alleluia, alleluia.

Then these refrains:

PRIEST: Give rest, O Lord, to the soul(s) of Thy servant(s) who hath (have) fallen asleep.

CHANTERS: Give rest, O Lord, to the soul(s) of Thy servant(s) who hath (have) fallen asleep.

PRIEST: Glory to the Father and to the Son and to the Holy Spirit.

CHANTERS: Both now and ever, and unto the ages of ages. Amen.

PRIEST: Give rest, O Lord, to the soul of Thy servant who hath fallen asleep.

CHANTERS: Give rest, O Lord, to the soul of Thy servant who hath fallen asleep.

PRIEST: We bless the Father, the Son, and the Holy Spirit: the Lord.

CHANTERS: Both now and ever, and unto the ages of ages. Amen.

PRIEST: Give rest, O Lord, to the soul of Thy servant who hath fallen asleep.

CHANTERS: Give rest, O Lord, to the soul of Thy servant who hath fallen asleep.

PRIEST: Glory to the Father, and to the Son, and to the Holy Spirit.

CHANTERS: Both now and ever, and unto the ages of ages. Amen.

Then:

DEACON: The Theotokos and Mother of the Light let us magnify in song.

CHANTERS: The spirits and the souls of the righteous praise Thee, O Lord.

The Eirmos, Ode IX:

It is not possible for men to see God, upon Whom the ranks of angels dare not gaze; but through Thee, O All-pure One, appeared to men the Word Incarnate, Whom magnifying, with the heavenly hosts we call Thee blessed.

READER: Holy God, Holy Mighty, Holy Immortal, have mercy on us. *Thrice.*

Glory to the Father, and to the Son, and to the Holy Spirit, both now and ever, and unto the ages of ages. Amen.

O Most Holy Trinity, have mercy on us. O Lord, blot out our sins. O Master, pardon our iniquities. O Holy One, visit and heal our infirmities for Thy name's sake.

Lord, have mercy. *Thrice.*

Glory to the Father, and to the Son, and to

the Holy Spirit, both now and ever, and unto the ages of ages. Amen.

Our Father, Who art in the heavens, hallowed be Thy name. Thy kingdom come, Thy will be done, on earth as it is in heaven. Give us this day our daily bread, and forgive us our debts, as we forgive our debtors; and lead us not into temptation, but deliver us from the evil one.

PRIEST: For Thine is the kingdom, and the power, and the glory, of the Father and of the Son and of the Holy Spirit, now and ever, and unto the ages of ages.

CHANTERS: Amen.

Then these troparia, 4th Tone:

With the souls of the righteous that have finished their course, give rest, O Saviour, to the soul(s) of Thy servant(s), preserving his/her (them) in the blessed life which is with Thee, O Lover of mankind.

In the place of Thy rest, O Lord, where all

Thy saints repose, give rest also to the soul(s) of Thy servant(s), for Thou alone art the Lover of Mankind.

Glory to the Father and to the Son and to the Holy Spirit.

Thou art the God Who descended into hades and loosed the chains of the captives; do Thou Thyself give rest also to the soul(s) of Thy servant(s).

Both now and ever, and unto the ages of ages. Amen.

O only pure and blameless Virgin, Who without seed gavest birth to God, pray that his/her (their) soul(s) be saved.

Then the Litany:

DEACON: Have mercy on us, O God, according to Thy great mercy, we pray Thee, hearken and have mercy.

CHANTERS: Lord, have mercy. *Thrice.*

DEACON: Again we pray for the repose of the soul(s) of the departed servant(s) of God

(*N.*), and that they (or, he/she) may be forgiven every transgression, both voluntary and involuntary.

CHANTERS: Lord, have mercy. *Thrice.*

DEACON: That the Lord God commit their souls to where the righteous repose.

CHANTERS: Lord, have mercy. *Thrice.*

DEACON: The mercy of God, the kingdom of heaven, and the remission of their sins, let us ask of Christ, the Immortal King and our God.

CHANTERS: Grant this, O Lord.

DEACON: Let us pray to the Lord.

CHANTERS: Lord, have mercy.

The priest says this prayer secretly:

O God of spirits and of all flesh, Who hast trampled down death, and overthrown the devil, and given life to Thy world: do Thou Thyself, O Lord, give rest to the soul(*s*) of Thy departed servant(*s*) (*N.*), in a place of light, a place of green pasture, a place of repose, whence all sickness, sorrow and sighing are fled away. Pardon every sin committed by his/her (them) in word, deed, or thought, in that Thou art a good God, the Lover of mankind; for there is no man that liveth and sinneth not, for Thou alone art without sin, Thy righteousness is an everlasting righteousness, and Thy word is truth.

EXCLAMATION: For Thou art the resurrection, and the life, and the repose of Thy departed servant*(s)* (*N.*), O Christ our God, and unto Thee do we send up glory, together with Thine unoriginate Father, and Thy most holy and good and life-creating Spirit, now and ever, and unto the ages of ages.

CHANTERS: Amen.

DEACON: Wisdom!

PRIEST: O Most Holy Theotokos, save us!

CHANTERS: More honorable than the Cherubim, and beyond compare more glorious than the Seraphim, Who without corruption gavest birth to God the Word, the very Theotokos, Thee do we magnify.

PRIEST: Glory to Thee, O Christ God, our hope, glory to Thee.

CHANTERS: Glory to the Father and to the Son and to the Holy Spirit, both now and ever, and unto the ages of ages. Amen.

Lord, have mercy. *Thrice.*

Father (Master), bless.

The Dismissal

PRIEST: May Christ our true God, Who rose from the dead, through the intercessions of His most pure Mother, of the holy and all-praised apostles, of our holy and God-bearing fathers, and of all the saints, commit the soul(s) of His servant(s) that hath/have departed from us, (*N.*), to the tabernacles of the righteous, give him/her (them) rest in the bosom of Abraham, and number him/her (them) with the righteous, and have mercy on us, for He is good and the Lover of mankind.

CHANTERS: Amen.

DEACON: In a blessed falling asleep, grant, O Lord, eternal rest unto Thy departed servant(s) (*N.*), and make his/her (their) memory to be eternal.

CHANTERS: Memory Eternal. *Thrice.*

PRIEST: May God bless and give him/her (them) rest, and have mercy on us, for He is good and the Lover of mankind.

CHANTERS: Amen.

A Prayer for Every Departed Person

Remember, O Lord our God, Thy servant (handmaiden) who hath departed in the faith and hope of eternal life, our brother (sister), (*N.*), and, as Thou art good and lovest mankind, pardon his/her sins and consume his/her unrighteousness; release, remit and forgive all his/her sins, voluntary and involuntary. Deliver him/her from eternal torment and from the fire of Gehenna, and grant unto him/her participation and enjoyment of Thine eternal blessings, which have been prepared for them that love Thee. For if he/she sinned, yet he/she did not renounce Thee and believed undoubtingly in Thee as God: the Father, the Son, and the Holy Spirit, glorified in Trinity, and confessed the Unity in Trinity and the Trinity in Unity in Orthodox

fashion, even until his/her last breath. Therefore, be merciful unto him/her and impute
his/her faith in Thee instead of deeds and, as
One gracious, grant unto him/her rest with
Thy saints. For there is no man who liveth and
sinneth not, and Thou only art without sin,
and Thy righteousness is righteousness for
ever. For Thou alone art a God of mercy, and
compassion, and love for mankind, and unto
Thee do we ascribe glory, to the Father, and to
the Son, and to the Holy Spirit; now, and ever,
and unto the ages of ages. Amen.

PART 3

Prayer List for the Health and Salvation of the Servants of God

_____

_____

_____

_____

_____

_____

_____

_____

_____

_____

_____

_____

_____

_____

_____

_____

_____

_____

_____

Prayer List for the Repose
of the Servants of God

_____

_____

_____

_____

_____

_____

_____

_____

_____

_____

_____

_____

_____

_____

_____

_____

_____

_____

_____